To The People
—GH

And For Our Families
—CM & BM

ABCD
EFGHIJ
KLMNO
PQRSTU
VyWX
YZ

Gerald Hausman

TURTLE ISLAND ABC

A GATHERING OF
NATIVE AMERICAN SYMBOLS

Illustrated by
Cara and Barry Moser

HarperCollinsPublishers

INTRODUCTION

Christopher Columbus, sailing across the Atlantic from Spain in 1492, thought he had come to the East Indies, or India. His first landfall was the Bahamian island of San Salvador in the Caribbean. The people he saw there he called *Indios*, or Indians, because he thought he had come to the East—to India or Asia. But he had not—he had come to the West . . . to what would soon be called the New World.

The people whom Columbus called Indians referred to themselves, in their own languages, as The People. The largest island on which they lived—North America—they named Turtle Island.

The turtle, an ancient creature, was believed to be sacred. The People told stories of how the first turtle carried the land on her back. They told of how Beaver packed mud on Turtle's back and made the land that is now North America.

How did Turtle Island become North America?

It was named after Americus Vespucius, an Italian merchant who came along after Columbus had made his "discovery." Naturally, this name was not chosen by The People, who had been living on Turtle Island for thousands of years.

The People thought land was more precious than the gold sought by Columbus and his men. It was sacred. They named the land Turtle Island, but the whole earth they called Mother Earth. For she was like their mother, kind and protective and strong. The sun was called Father Sun, watchful and covering all. Together, Mother Earth and Father Sun looked after The People. And they, in return, looked after them.

Today, much has been lost of these old ways of thinking. But The People still hold their beliefs. The old turtle, they say, is alive and well, still toting us on her back. Although the burden she carries is greater than it once was—because there are so many people to carry—she is very strong.

This book tells the story of the things the old turtle carries on her back. These are words, definitions; and they are told as stories in The People's way. Each thing the old turtle carries is part of a tradition that is alive today, a tradition passed down from generation to generation.

The arrow, for instance, is not merely a weapon for killing. It is also a way of sending a prayer to Sun Father. The drum is not just a musical instrument. It, too, can send messages; and it reminds The People of the heartbeat of Mother Earth.

All of the words in *Turtle Island ABC* are common ones because they come from common ground. The People have been sharing them with us since the beginning, since our first meeting on Turtle Island. If we have another, closer look at them, perhaps we will know how much The People have given us.

Gerald Hausman
Tesuque, New Mexico

A
ARROW

I am the ARROW that is sent from a bow. ❖ I am strong and straight. The People sing a prayer as they send me into the sky. I go straight up, carrying The People's prayer for rain. Soon clouds come, and the rain begins to fall, and the crops begin to grow. ❖ I am the arrow that is sent from a bow.

B

BUFFALO

I am the big-horned BUFFALO of the plains. ❖ Where I go, the grass lies down. Once, long ago, I ran and swam and grazed all over Turtle Island. The People lived beside me in their tipis. We sang many songs together. I showed The People how to be strong, and they made their leaders into Buffalo Chiefs. ❖ I am the big-horned buffalo of the plains.

C
CORN

I am the CORN known as First Food. ❖ Yellow corn, The People say, stands like a good mother, holding her child. White corn, they say, stands still like a strong father, watching over his family. With Mother Earth's breath and Sun Father's warmth, I grow, and my kernels are the colors of the rainbow: white, yellow, red, and blue. ❖ I am the corn known as First Food.

I am the DRUM The People play when they dance and sing. ❖ They say I sound like a heartbeat. Ba-boom, ba-boom. I keep a steady beat when The People play upon my skin. I keep time for the dancers' moccasin feet as they lift and fall to my steady beat. ❖ I am the drum The People play when they dance and sing.

E

EAGLE

I am EAGLE, the strongest bird in the sky. ❖ Once, long ago, I took one of The People, a little boy, into the sky-world, and he met all of the Eagle People there. I showed him how to do the Eagle Dance, which brings eagle-strength into everyone's life. Today, The People still dance in my honor. They sing and dance and wear my feathers. ❖ I am Eagle, the strongest bird in the sky.

F
FEATHER

I am the FEATHER that travels on the wind. ❖ They make me into coats and hats, blankets and masks. I take messages The People give me, and I carry them to Wind, Rainbow, and Sun. I act as a messenger from Mother Earth to Father Sun. If you have a special wish, I will carry it for you. ❖ I am the feather that travels on the wind.

G

GREAT SERPENT

I am GREAT SERPENT, who lives in the earth. ❖ I guide and protect all of the Snake People. With my power to protect, I can make thunder and lightning. The People say that I have deer tracks on my back, and that I smell like rain. They say I have no arms or legs because I lost them, long ago, during the Great Flood. Now I can move swiftly, like a cloud. ❖ I am Great Serpent, who lives in the earth.

H

HUMMINGBIRD

I am HUMMINGBIRD, the medicine man. ❖ I ring a little bell when I come around to visit. I make all the other birds well. I fill acorn shells with medicine that I make from dewdrops. I sing the old, old songs that The People have forgotten. ❖ I am Hummingbird, the medicine man.

I

INDIAN

I am the INDIAN, who is a child of Earth and Sun. ❖ Once, so they say, we came out of the ground. And once, we fell out of the sky. And once, they tell us, we were even planted in the ground, and grew like corn. But no matter where we came from, we know what we are. We are a part of the breath of all things that live. ❖ I am the Indian, who is a child of Earth and Sun.

J

JAR

I am the JAR, made of clay from Mother Earth. ❖ If I fall and break, you can pick me up, grind me into dust, shape me back into clay, and make me all over again. ❖ I am the jar, made of clay from Mother Earth.

K

KACHINA

I am the KACHINA, made from the branch of a cottonwood tree.
❖ Long ago, The People lived in the underworld, which is the belly of the earth. The kachinas lived with them there and taught them many things. The kachinas taught The People how to live, how to be thankful for all that is good. And The People never forgot. That is why they still carve kachina dolls out of wood and give them to their children. ❖ I am the kachina, made from the branch of a cottonwood tree.

L

LIGHT

I am the LIGHT that comes from the sun, moon, and stars. ❖ I warm your hands on a cold winter morning. I help you make your way home in the dark. Although you may not notice me, I am always around. Look into your very own eye—a small, smiling light. ❖ I am the light that comes from the sun, moon, and stars.

M

MOTHER EARTH

I am MOTHER EARTH. ❖ I care for The People, for I am their mother. When they think of the earth under their feet, they think of me. When it rains, they say I have let down my long hair. When it snows, they say I have put on my white winter dress. They know that each season I change my clothes. But I am always the same. ❖ I am Mother Earth.

N
NAME

I am the NAME that a person is given. ❖ *Wind Boy*, the name given to a boy with the wind in his hair. *Dawn Girl*, the name given to a girl who runs toward the dawn. I am what someone was, what someone is, what someone will become. ❖ I am the name that a person is given.

O

OWL

I am OWL, bird of the night. ❖ Once, so they say, I raised a boy, and taught him to be an owl. I showed him how to see at night and how to ride the wind. They say my boy lives deep in the forest because he is shy of being with The People. You can hear him call on dark nights: "Who, who, who goes there?" ❖ I am Owl, bird of the night.

P

PUEBLO

I am the PUEBLO, the house made of many houses. ❖ The People shape me out of mud, brick, and straw. They make rooms, one on top of the other. They say I am warm in winter and cool in summer. Long ago, when the first Spanish explorers saw me, they thought I was made of gold. But it was just the sun that painted me gold. ❖ I am the pueblo, the house made of many houses.

QUARTZ

I am QUARTZ, the bright crystal stone. ❖ White, pink, gray, and blue, I shine in the sun and sparkle in the moon. Medicine men use me to heal the sick. They hold me up to the sun or the moon and watch the colors that come out of me. From these colors they can tell what medicine to make to help someone get well. ❖ I am Quartz, the bright crystal stone.

I am ROUND, the shape of all good things. ❖ The People say that goodness is round: round, the sun-shaped basket; round, the moon-shaped bracelet. Round, the dance The People do; round, the lodge they live in. Round is the world and the word *round*. ❖ I am Round, the shape of all good things.

S

SUN FATHER

I am SUN FATHER. ❖ The People say that I ride four different horses. These are for the different colors of the sky that I light up as I ride by during the day. First, I ride on a white-shell horse in the morning. Then, I ride on a turquoise horse in the afternoon. Then, I ride on a red-shell horse at sunset. Last, I ride on a jet-black horse at night. ❖ I am Sun Father.

T

TURTLE ISLAND

I am TURTLE ISLAND. ❖ The People tell of the time long ago when the land was formed from the Great Sea. They say there were only water animals then. Beaver scooped up mud with his tail and patted it on my back, and they say this was The People's first home. I am old, but ever young. ❖ I am Turtle Island.

U
UNDERWORLD

I am the UNDERWORLD, the belly of the earth. ❖ The People say that First Man and First Woman came out of me. They say I am a place of water, fire, air, and earth. I am the place of first breath and first birth. Where I am, it is dark, and quiet. But it is not empty. Things begin in me: rivers and mountains, men and women. ❖ I am the underworld, the belly of the earth.

V

VOICE

I am the VOICE of The People raised in song. ❖ Many tribes, many nations come together and make themselves into one song, one voice. Now I am many voices, singing as one person. I sing like the wind in the grass and the rain in the trees. I sing like a man, a mouse, a mountain lion. ❖ I am the voice of The People raised in song.

W

WOLF

I am WOLF, the big wanderer who went away. ❖ Long ago, so The People say, I was sent to learn the secret of the dawn. I stayed away a long time, wandering. On my long legs, I went to far places. When I came back, I still did not know the secret of the dawn. ❖ I am Wolf, the big wanderer who went away.

X

X

I am the CROSSING PLACE. ❖ Where two trails meet, going their separate ways, I am there. Where two rivers cross, where two mountains meet, where The People put down their packs, I am there. I am the place where they rest and the place where they go on. Draw half of me, and I am just a falling line. Put me together with my other half, and I am a pretty design. ❖ I am the crossing place.

Y

YUCCA

I am the YUCCA plant, who lives in the desert. ❖ Long ago The People made me into sandals and used the string of my leaves to tie up bundles. They dug up my root and made me into shampoo for their hair. I am a spiky poker, a sun-loving loafer who lives on hills of fine blown sand. The People still use me to make their hair shine in the sun. ❖ I am the yucca plant, who lives in the desert.

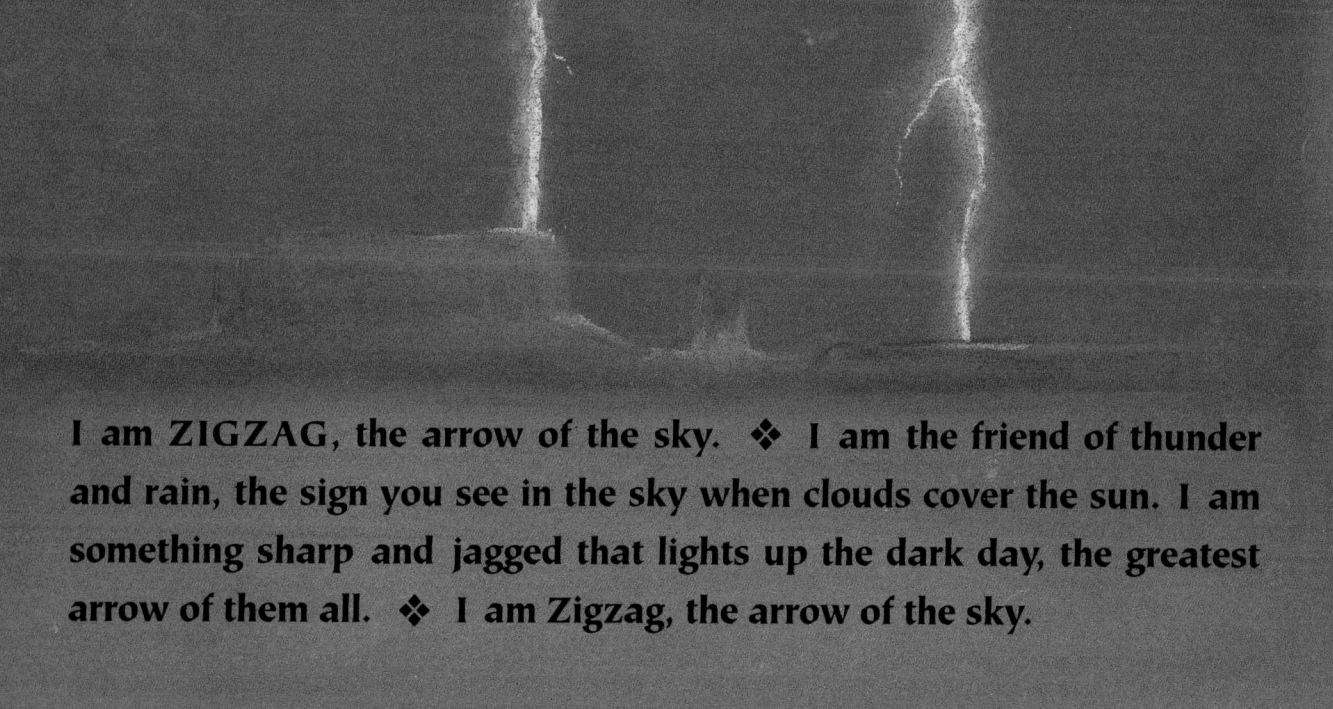

Z

ZIGZAG

I am ZIGZAG, the arrow of the sky. ❖ I am the friend of thunder and rain, the sign you see in the sky when clouds cover the sun. I am something sharp and jagged that lights up the dark day, the greatest arrow of them all. ❖ I am Zigzag, the arrow of the sky.

The text display type for
Turtle Island ABC: *A Gathering of Native American Symbols*
was composed in Tiepolo.
The paintings were executed in pastel on board.
The transparencies were made by
Gamma One Conversions, New York, New York.
The color separations were made by Imago/Bright Arts.
The entire book was printed by Worzalla
on 80# Patina made by S.D. Warren Company.
Bound by Worzalla.
Production supervision by Erin Dwyer.
Designed by Barry Moser, Cara Moser, and Christine Kettner.

Turtle Island ABC
A Gathering of Native American Symbols
Text copyright © 1994 by Gerald Hausman
Illustrations copyright © 1994 by Cara Moser

Library of Congress Cataloging-in-Publication Data
Hausman, Gerald.
    Turtle Island ABC: a gathering of Native American symbols /
by Gerald Hausman ; illustrated by Cara and Barry Moser.
        p.   cm.
    Summary: An alphabet book of traditional Native American symbols.
    ISBN 0-06-021307-8. — ISBN 0-06-021308-6 (lib. bdg.)
    1. Indians of North America—Juvenile literature.
2. Alphabet—Juvenile literature.   3. Signs and symbols—Juvenile literature.
[1. Indians of North America.   2. Alphabet.
3. Signs and symbols.]   I. Moser, Cara, ill.   II. Moser, Barry, ill.
III. Title.
E77.4.H38   1994   92-14982
497—dc20   CIP
[E]   AC